MARBLE IN METAMORPHOSIS

MARBLE IN METAMORPHOSIS

Essay by Rachel Cusk
Photography by Chris Kontos

Published by Molonglo

Previous Page:
The island of Tinos in the Cyclades, 2018

Μυθιστόρημα, ΚΑ'
Του Γιώργου Σεφέρη

Ἐμεῖς ποὺ ξεκινήσαμε γιὰ τὸ προσκύνημα τοῦτο
κοιτάξαμε τὰ σπασμένα ἀγάλματα
ξεχαστήκαμε καὶ εἴπαμε πὼς δὲ χάνεται ἡ ζωὴ τόσο εὔκολα
πὼς ἔχει ὁ θάνατος δρόμους ἀνεξερεύνητους
καὶ μία δική του δικαιοσύνη

πὼς ὅταν ἐμεῖς ὀρθοὶ στὰ πόδια μας πεθαίνουμε
μέσα στὴν πέτρα ἀδερφωμένοι
ἑνωμένοι μὲ τὴ σκληρότητα καὶ τὴν ἀδυναμία,
οἱ παλαιοὶ νεκροὶ ξεφύγαν ἀπ' τὸν κύκλο καὶ ἀναστήθηκαν
καὶ χαμογελᾶνε μέσα σὲ μία παράξενη ἡσυχία.

Mythistorema, 21
By George Seferis
Translated by Edmund Keeley

We who set out on this pilgrimage
looked at the broken statues
became distracted and said that life is not so easily lost
that death has unexplored paths
and its own particular justice;

that while we, still upright on our feet, are dying,
affiliated in stone
united in hardness and weakness,
the ancient dead have escaped the circle and risen again
and smile in a strange silence.

CONTENTS

11
MARBLE IN METAMORPHOSIS
RACHEL CUSK

31
TINOS
CHRIS KONTOS

85
ATHENS
CHRIS KONTOS

131
AFTERWORD
NADINE MONEM

MARBLE IN METAMORPHOSIS
RACHEL CUSK

It is spring, but the village shows no sign of awakening. It has an atmosphere of changelessness that borders on indifference. The village is an environment that is tolerant of – rather than mastered by – the human. Here and there ruined buildings, their windows dark cavities, sit among the white houses – themselves frequently in various states of disrepair – that climb the hill and overlook the bay. These signs of decay are like tidemarks of human effort, from which the propulsive force of will has long since receded. The landscape these structures once sought to complement is that to which now they are surrendering themselves. It is a painless, gentle kind of extinguishing that occurs in surroundings of such natural beauty, more of a return than a death. Occasionally a tall tree can be seen growing through a collapsed roof. The sounds of birds and animals and insects fill the air. Now and then a fishing boat slowly crosses the bay in the falling darkness, ploughing a thick, luxurious furrow across the pale water. An arrival is also a change of palette, of materials. The white rectilinear shapes of the village ascending the dry rocky hillside, the dusty stillness of the lanes in the blue light of evening, the motionless sea, milk-coloured as it absorbs the last light: these tones and textures of Greece, so instantly recognisable, are nonetheless a sensory shock after the grey turbulence of a northern winter.

The house, woken from its winter sleep, remains immersed in its own memories. It is full of old books and ornaments and photographs; the large, dark rooms are like theatre sets for a drama that has long since concluded. In the entrance hall there is a piece of marble in a frame, hung on the wall like a painting. It is a highly polished rectangular slab, embedded with small sparkling ammonites and fossils linked by great spidery tracings and arcs against a dark background, so that from a distance it resembles a galaxy looked at through a telescope. Its presence in a frame is a statement of some kind. The piece of marble is no more a painting than nature itself is a painting, yet like a painting it speaks for itself: it is complete. It is separated from the process of its own becoming and can stand apart. It is also a narrative of sorts, a story of time, though one with neither protagonist nor author – a very impartial kind of witness, this framed piece of marble, that is being given an opportunity to testify.

The house generally is in a state of semi-dereliction, for the owner never comes here, to this village on a Greek hillside by the sea. In other climates the weather would quickly have invaded and destroyed the building, but here its decay has a sort of grace, is a mere note on the scale of its likewise decaying neighbours, a kind of collective, noiseless fading out under the oblivious eye of the sun. From the evidence of those houses, the roof with its wooden trusses will be the first to go; then the floors, made of narrow blackened boards, which already feel doubtful underfoot. When the wind blows and the old doors and windows flap and bang, the floor gives a great swaying lurch, as though it is beginning to detach itself from the two-foot-thick stone walls. Those walls are stubborn and will deteriorate at their own aloof, imperceptible rate. Long cracks run along the cement walls enclosing the terrace. The garden is faded and overgrown, and old patterns of human habitation can be discerned there, a broken arbour collapsing under its greenery, a rusting table and chairs placed in the shade of an unruly tree. Anything made of fabric has long since bleached and rotted away. What these materials say is that human intentions must be subject to time: unless the bond with them is continually renewed, the vow to those intentions re-sworn, they will not be permitted to last. The two-foot-thick walls are a kind of ballast against this prospect: they are an inheritance, which the neglect of the wooden floors and roof is squandering. In order to survive, this house – so full of the memory of the dead or departed – requires a new partnership with the living.

The piece of marble, of course, is completely intact, though the frame – being made of wood – is starting to come apart. There is a marble slab in the garden too, used as a tabletop: it gleams, white and indifferent, in the dusk that falls over that untended little wilderness. Unaffected by the general atmosphere of decay, its survival is almost a form of vulnerability. Because it can't die, it has no story to tell. A long time ago it was taken out of the earth and shaped by a forgotten human hand, and now it sits here in this garden, recording nothing.

***

Marble, the metamorphic rock, embodies a dark paradox: it is change that produces changelessness. Over time, subjected to the geological forces of intense heat and compression beneath the earth's surface, limestone recrystallises and becomes more durable. An alteration of character occurs, a metamorphosis that is a response to extremes. The result is a loss of fallibility, of weakness. One might almost say that the rock's sufferings, its experience, bring about its immortality.

According to the human idea, not to change is to die. Death is the changeless state; yet change is resisted all the same, because it also represents loss. It is comforting to find something that is unchanged, that has lasted. Through the things that have lasted our ancestors seem to speak to us and to offer us their reassurance. The relic, the Renaissance masterpiece, the castle or cathedral are all eroded by time and context yet their authority – even while its meaning might alter or be lost – is retained. A constraint is likewise exercised by what has lasted: this quality of lastingness, so difficult to achieve in our own endeavours, can give rise to the notion that it is better to go backwards than to go forwards, that what is new is to be feared and what is safest and most reliable about ourselves is already behind us.

What makes certain things last, while others decay and are forgotten? Perhaps what lasts is what continues to fit into the human story, what we can bend to our subjective understanding of who we are. For something to last we have to continue to agree with it, even if what we are agreeing with is something the lasting object never intended. Time strips an object of its context, revealing it for the achievement or mistake that it was, but what becomes of its intentions? One might say that an artist is a person who has found a way to bind their intentions to the object they create. Yet how can they know whether those intentions will or ought to last?

The ethos of marble is endurance, and as such it has no particular morality of its own. It represents a concept of change that is difficult to grasp. As a material marble lies outside any given moment: having already changed, and thereby become changeless, it is no longer subject to time. It speaks to us not as individuals but as participants in an ongoing history. It reminds us of the impermanence that underlies these individual possessions of ours, these bodies, these selves, and asks us to ally ourselves with something more collective and enduring. Do we wish to endure? In marble we could inscribe what we wish of ourselves to endure: marble is a material for a pure and almost a monomaniacal intention. The survival of marble, like the survival of certain memories while others vanish, is likewise a kind of subjectivity. A story is made out of what survives. Other ways in which stories are told – the stories of influence and becoming, of unconscious action and belief, moral and oral histories – do not have a location as resilient as that of marble. They can be influenced or modified; they can evolve, or dwindle away. To an extent a story is made out of the juncture between the immaterial and the material. In marble the distance between the two – between fleetingness and survival, between expressiveness and dumbness – is immense. So much of what we do is forgotten or isn't good enough. So who can be the author of this material?

***

The village ought to be a quiet place, yet every day the air is filled with the noise of building work. The old houses are being refurbished by newcomers, people with vision and money. At the house directly behind ours, a group of men are blasting out an area of hillside to uncover the remains of another building that apparently are buried on its land. We have been told that this is a common ruse among property developers, since it is difficult here to get permission to build something new. The rubble they are digging for is merely the justification of their intentions, which are to put up two new houses that can be sold for profit. Every morning shortly after sunrise they start their pneumatic drill and spend the day breaking up the hard rock underfoot. On the first day, dismayed by the deafening noise, we walked around to the house to talk to its owner, an American with a distinctly unrepentant manner, who told us that the drilling was likely to continue for the whole extent of our stay. He outlined for us the history and progress of these works, which began with the felling of all the trees on the site, followed by a period of exploration, in which the men dug at the hillside with shovels in the hope of striking – as it were – gold. Once they had ascertained that the remains were there, the American had applied for a permit, which had taken some time to come through. Now that he had it, he was not about to desist on our account. Find somewhere else to stay, he said imperiously – it'd be the cleanest thing. Later he offered us lettuces from his vegetable garden, and a bottle of olive oil, and seemed satisfied that he had evened things out. Every lunchtime we eat the prospector's lettuce, garnished with a few drops of his olive oil, shouting at one another above the noise.

I have often considered the merits of insensitivity, and thought how much better it would be not to be continually pained by the activities of other humans, even at the cost of losing what might be distinctive about oneself. But in fact the building work is a simple exercise in perspective: were I in the American's shoes, perhaps I would be doing the same thing. Most people live cosseted in the vague belief that their existence and the work that they do are essentially non-destructive, but hardly anyone in our era can really say that about themselves. These days, the very condition of being alive represents an act of extortion: it is unavoidable. The American is merely making his extortion audible and visible. Unlike him, the men who are doing the work are local: I watch them from the garden, unable to understand their talk and so reading instead their mannerisms and gestures, their bearing toward one other and their employer. They seem gentle and respectful. They aren't responsible for the destruction and the noise, yet these things, and the change that will result from them, are their work.

Two things – beauty and horror – are especially lasting, and in the built environment they frequently come intertwined. The grandiosity of marble, for instance, bequeathed it by classicism and religion, easily becomes the grandiosity of fascism. Looking at images of the Palace of the Parliament in Bucharest – the world's heaviest building, so heavy that it sinks six millimetres into the earth every year – it is hard not to see in it a tremendous spectacle of wrongful labour. It is a colossus that represents the translation of a dictator's will into a physical and spatial reality. Other feats of building and engineering – the nearby strait of Corinth, for instance – are triumphs of human will whose fathomless cost in physical toil is impossible to ignore: a kind of uneasiness attends these marvels, which remind us how far progress has relied on the existence of inequality. The Palace of the Parliament seems to ask a different question, which is a question about the moral status of oppression: can a person in a state of oppression be deemed blameless for his or her acts? The building of this pointless edifice entailed the displacement of 40,000 residents of Bucharest and the demolition of an entire quarter of the city that also housed monasteries, libraries and museums. Over a million cubic metres of marble were used in the construction. The men who built it were not labourers or soldiers: they were termed 'volunteers', the question of their will thus being conveniently settled. It was a compulsory sort of volunteering, however: in fact they were little more than slaves. The palace is the world's third-largest building, yet fewer than half of its thousand-plus rooms were ever completed. It is an image of the suddenness with which a dictator's power can be extinguished.

The artist and the dictator stand at opposite ends of the concept of agreement, which is essentially the concept of storytelling. As a story does, the created object seeks agreement: unless successive generations agree with the statement the object makes, it will be destroyed by time. The artist makes a bet on that future perspective, even at the cost of dispensing with agreement in the now. By contrast, the dictator tries to stop time and control the future, by staking everything on the present moment. Where the artist is often weaker than the things he creates, the dictator struggles to create something that will outlast him. Yet both are bent on commemorating their vision by embodying it in that which exists outside themselves, that which is concrete.

The artists and dictators of our time are increasingly interested in immateriality: the new forms of power are digital, the new art an art that doesn't rely on concretisation. When the artist Michael Landy publicly destroyed everything he owned, including works he possessed by other artists, he was making a statement about the hopeless corruption of the object world, from which art must attempt to separate itself. The British artist Andy Goldsworthy often makes works whose substance is the simple act of perception: uncoupled from representation, they are embodied in the object-value of what is seen, to whose fleetingness the artist surrenders. Goldsworthy's art could be termed non-egotistical, since its materials belong to and can be recouped by nature: it is an art of minimal interference, of non-competition, one which, theoretically at least, permits anyone to be an artist. It is resistant to dogma and misinterpretation, yet is it also perhaps resistant to responsibility? By creating a lasting object, the artist takes responsibility for those who look at it, now and into the future. He believes he can communicate with those future people, and reassure them that their surmises about the world and its truth are the same as his own. Michelangelo, famous egotist, regarded marble as the most formidable of all prisons of the human idea. "The greatest artist has no conception," he is quoted as saying, "which a single block of marble does not potentially contain within its mass, but only a hand obedient to the mind can penetrate to this image." Liberating the image from its confinement in the material is a supreme act of human domination, is to stamp existence on the most indifferent and immortal of stones. What this domination relies on – like all domination – is obedience, the obedience of the self, the hand, to the mind's intentions. Michelangelo's hand is his slave, like the actual slave of the dictator, bent to a will outside itself. For the human idea doesn't only extend to truth and beauty: if the block of marble contains all ideas, all conceptions, it is equally full of evil.

***

In the news there is the story of the release of the Torlonia marbles, a hoard of more than six hundred statues belonging to a family of Italian aristocrats. They had once been housed in the enormous family museum at Trastevere, where only people whose names appeared in the Golden Book of Italian Nobility were permitted to visit them. But in the 1960s, apparently, the family applied for a permit to repair the museum's roof, whereupon they proceeded to convert the building into ninety three apartments, behind the cover of a gigantic opaque construction fence. The six hundred statues were crammed into three storage rooms, where investigators reported they were "stacked on top of each other like junk". The government's attempts to rescue the collection began to bear fruit only when the incumbent duke finally died at the age of ninety two, and a portion of the statues were released to the Capitoline Museum in Rome.

The survival of the human gesture, in art, is intricately bound to the capacity of its materials to survive: the appropriation of artworks, in other times and places, has ensured their longevity. The Earl of Elgin, removing the marble friezes from the Parthenon and taking them home with him to England, claimed to have done so for their own safety: now they sit in the British Museum, captives of a different kind, estranged. Their stories and images can't be ended or erased but must continue to speak for eternity in their imprisonment. A question of trust has become a question of power. Is ownership of an artist's work equal to the ownership of their intentions? Does a work 'belong' to its people, to its country? The essence of the artist's gesture is freedom, freedom from every context and condition, freedom even from the parts of his own identity that have arisen out of that context. There are societies who persecute their artists, for whom the survival of an artist's intentions can become, later on, an opportunity for justice. The piling up of the statues in the storeroom, unseen, is merely a great silencing. The Torlonian story is a story of the stubborn persistence of materials, through which human indifference or greed continue to wage war against expressive truth. In marble, the human gesture is conserved against attrition and attack. It can survive the silencing and still retain the capacity to speak.

Not far from the Capitoline Museum is the Foro Italico, the gigantic sports complex built by Mussolini in the 1930s as a temple to fascist principles of manhood. Today football fans come and go beneath its marble porticoes, past the mock-classical statues of athletes, past the huge marble obelisk Mussolini erected in honour of himself. The Olympic Games were held there in 1960, and it continues to be regularly used for international sporting events: despite the malevolence of its architectural statement, it seems it is too well-made and convenient a structure for anyone to have considered knocking it down. In the nearby Colosseum, tourists are safe to ponder the far-off days when humans were fed to lions for sport. The continuing functionality of Mussolini's stadium retains an insidiousness that would be difficult to quantify because it has not yet been exhausted. Like the statues in the storeroom, the intentions of the maker are conserved in the durability of marble. There is a theory that the stadium – along with the similar stadia Mussolini built in other Italian cities – played a central role in the evolution of Italian football from a parochial sport to the profitable, competitive and morally ambiguous phenomenon it has become in the modern era. Rome, that built environment Freud likened to the human self, with all its memories and defining epochs standing amid the buzz and sprawl of the present day, is a place where the question of influence – the idea that we ourselves might be shaped by concrete things – continually arises. Can we gauge the influence on ourselves of the things that surround us if we no longer remember what they mean?

At the museum, the whiteness of marble is enshrined: the pale forms radiate what seems to be purity, the purity of a past so deep and distant it has shed the colours and textures of living, has shed its links with the now. They are like solid ghosts, these statues of men and women and gods and animals. Silent though they are, they appear to speak. Yet their message is too cryptic: perhaps it is the case that, their meaning having been fundamentally lost to us, we read into them what we want to read.

In their time, the marble figures of Greek antiquity were gaudily painted: the cold perfection of their whiteness, their suggestion of eternity, is perversely unrepresentative. Stripped of colour, what they inadvertently bequeathed to the world were notions of classicism that appeared to repudiate reality and nature, suggesting instead an inorganic ideal of perfectibility. "What a scandal to hear nature deprecated in comparison to Greek statues," Goya wrote, referring to the new teaching of art in formal academies. The struggle of art became the struggle to move forward against the tether of antiquity, to represent movement and life. The marble ideal was left to the preserve of conservatism, embodying a resistance to the new. Reborn into whiteness, with their colours washed away, the statues outlived their makers' intentions and lost their claim not to immortality but to its reverse – to the precious, pulsing truth of that which is mortal.

There is a curious reluctance to accept or admit that the sculpture of antiquity was colourful – it is a fact that is continuously subject to a collective cultural forgetting. Painted, the marble forms no longer represent perfection: it is as though the paint connects them to a fundamentally flawed humanity from which, through time, they have succeeded in distancing themselves. The presence of colour reasserts the non-ideal of reality and of individual human truth: it offers resistance to the appropriation of the white ideal by those who see in it the possibility of a humanity uncompromised by difference.

In the museum, there are numerous striking works of funerary decoration, in which the dead are shown in living scenes of marble relief, amid their familiars. Like photographs, these scenes seek to preserve the moment: imagining them in colour, they become suggestive of invocation rather than commemoration, of a desire to see the dead one alive again. There is an image of a mother adoringly nursing her baby, of a man talking and laughing among his companions, of two mature and handsome sisters sitting merrily side by side. The role of marble – to defeat death – suddenly appears in a new light: not an alternative to mortality, but a passionate testament to it.

***

We go to visit a quarry, where for centuries marble has been taken out of the earth. Along the road the villages become more and more marble-clad, as though this nearby opening of the earth had spattered them with its contents. The terrain rises into black vertiginous peaks: the villages cling to the steep hillsides, radiant white, rinsed by violent winds. The traditions and techniques of marble sculpting have been conserved here through successive generations. It is possible, we are told, for even an expert in these matters to fall into conversation with an old man in a local cafe and learn something new. In one of the larger villages there is a school where the art of marble sculpting is formally taught: the students' works-in-progress stand around the studio.

There is a block of marble there too, as yet untouched. A block of marble has a skin, beneath which its compacted layers become increasingly dense. It is composed of infinitesimal leaves, like a giant fine-paged book, that can easily be damaged. It is unexpectedly vulnerable: the students are taught to approach it with infinite caution. It can take as long as two years for them to shape a form from it, though an expert could do it in a month. The flash, the impulse of art would seem to be reined in – almost extinguished – by these conditions: the artist's gesture cannot be modified or retracted; their intentions, across this agonisingly slow creative process, cannot be altered. Rarely has the discipline, the un-freedom of art appeared more exacting – and indeed as art has sought over centuries to overcome the tension between discipline and creativity in order to produce change, inevitably the medium of marble has fallen deeper into conservatism. The new masters of marble – such as the students here will become – often find work as restorers, repairing and reassembling the broken forms of the ancient world that are always being raised up again from the earth.

Yet in the modern era certain artists are using marble as a location where a new ambivalence about history and power, about the meaning of the monumental, can be expressed. The Canadian artist Rebecca Belmore's marble replica of a cheap tent is an anti-monument, forcing the iconographic material into a dialogue with the state of displacement and homelessness. The Greek sculptor Andreas Lolis uses marble to create forms that represent the very concepts of disposability and waste: overstuffed bin bags, broken crates, crushed cardboard boxes. In Lolis' work, the relationship of time and forgetting to the durability of materials is turned inside out: here the medium is asked, painstakingly, to see that which is antithetical to itself, to notice what is beneath notice and commemorate it. Marble – the signifier of importance – is asked to bend itself to an act of recognition, the recognition of reality. Lolis' father was a stonemason: his relationship with marble began in childhood, when he slowly taught himself to make the material represent what he saw around him, against the formality of what was thought suitable to be seen. For other artists the technical difficulty of working in marble negates the possibility of using it as a medium. Belmore's tent, for instance, was carved by a graduate of the school here, in this village. Yet in the publicity surrounding that work, his name is nowhere mentioned. The art of marble carving has an uncertain status, just as it did when Michelangelo regarded his hand as his slave.

The quarry is a couple of miles out of the village, over a hillside facing the sea. The road rises, writhes through spurs of black rock and then plunges downward into the steep and savage landscape on the other side. It coils around the chasm-like mountainside with its dark and uninhabited vistas, the sea plunged far below. The great wound of the quarry appears some way down, along with other, older wounds: these belong to history, to the long account of human effort in plundering and shaping the world. In the nineteenth century the English quarried here, in a gash visible far down at the water's edge. By an almost maniacal feat of engineering, they even dug out the sea bed to quarry beneath the water. From the quarries higher up, the giant blocks of marble were manually handed down the mountainside, turned laboriously over from end to end.

It is evening, and the working quarry is deserted. Filthy trucks are parked here and there. The floor is a potholed mire of wet clay. The quarry is deep and steep-sided, its towering rectilinear façades at odds with the forms of nature: they look like the sides of buildings, as though the mountain already contained the idea of a city in its innards. Metres of rock and earth have to be blasted away to reach the marble below, and these layers are clearly visible on the exposed faces. The determination of man to reach the idea of a built environment, the idea of marble: even in the machine era, it is a scene of primitive struggle. One of the island's oldest marble sculptors has known this quarry since he was a boy: his father and grandfather were both quarrymen. In his earliest recollection it was a deep narrow channel cut into the earth. Now it is an arena, a brutal amphitheatre caked in mud and dust, facing the emptiness of sky and sea. As machines have come he has witnessed the diminution of toil here, which is also the ascent of human value. There has been a consequent loss of knowledge, of instinct: the great rough-cut blocks that stand around awaiting transportation elsewhere have to be clearly marked to show which is the right side up, because the quarry workers can no longer tell. The metamorphosis of which marble is the result comes about through pressure: if it is inverted it begins to lose its structural integrity. It is an image, in a way, of civilisation itself, the stress of its formation giving way to an ease which dismantles it, giving way to forgetting.

The story of marble's purity begins here, in the gradations and characteristics of the hewn-out mountainside. Intact, the façade is a kind of book, full of contrasts and passages of drama and colour, yet unintelligible and unshaped. In the editing process that follows this exposure of the material, the more consistent sections are preferred to the florid, wildly patinated ones. A particularly pale and unmarked face is the focus of current attention: it has been demarcated into slabs in preparation for cutting with long, fine copper cables studded with small diamonds that lie in great coils on the muddy ground. A few faint lines thread their way across the white façade, like tracks across snow. The discovery of this section has been the cause of excitement: it will make slabs of unusual size and quality. In the world of capitalism, white marble isn't just for monuments and dictators' palaces – it is a luxury material for the home. Cut to size, carefully polished and prepared, this lofty material, in which humans for centuries have inscribed their exceptionality and the grandeur of their vision, has finally been democratised.

***

A few miles from our house there are said to be the ruins of an ancient settlement. We have tried to find them before, but the paths are confusing. A dusty sign points from the road into a sloping valley of rocks and eucalyptus trees winding down toward the sea. The paths branch off in all directions, through mazes of dry stone walls separating small orchards of olive trees. These walls, we now realise, are the outskirts of the ancient city. We thread our way around them, climbing over broken sections, until we reach a broad paved way that runs parallel to the water. The Romans came here: this was once a busy harbour settlement of twenty-odd thousand people. Despite its size and importance it has been untouched by restoration. Instead it represents the truth of the history of human civilisation: it is a scene of abandonment. The handsome road made of huge worn slabs passes through towering landslides of broken stone heaped high on either side, through caved-in edifices, through the remains of cisterns and waterways, through carved arches and porticoes and pediments crushed beneath piles of rock. It winds graciously past the deserted harbour and up the steep hill on the other side, past a whole broken city that from a distance eerily resembles the quarry, the mountain in which man had found the human idea. Here that idea is returning to the earth, is echoing the forms of nature again. On the cliff at the top of the hill are the remains, just discernible, of a church: its crumbling archway, supported by a pillar, is more or less the last thing standing. Through the archway a dramatic vista of architectural collapse, almost like a waterfall of shale, can be seen. The sea pounds at the foot of the cliff far below. In the distance, from amid the grey cascade of stones, rise four slender white marble columns. They stand in a group, silent yet appearing to converse, four lonely survivors who continue to endure. In this dark, inchoate shingle landscape their whiteness is ethereal: they look like four fingers of light. Whatever purpose they served has long since vanished from their memories. They look patiently out to sea, waiting.

TINOS
CHRIS KONTOS

Marble quarry in Panormos on the island of Tinos, 2018

PREVIOUS PAGE:
Marble is mostly found in areas of extreme folding where continental and oceanic plates collide. These same areas produce earthquakes, volcanic activity and mountainous landscapes.

NEXT PAGE:
The life of marble begins deep inside the Earth, a metamorphic rock that forms when limestone is subjected to heat and pressure. Limestone's main component, recrystallised calcite, changes the texture of the rock. Early in the process, the calcite crystals are small. As metamorphism progresses, the crystals grow larger, erasing the fossils and sediments that once formed the limestone.

Marble wall at the Panormos quarry, 2018

A long view of the marble quarry in Panormos, 2018

PREVIOUS SPREAD:
The recrystallised calcite in marble mixes with other minerals that give different stones their colour. Clay, mica, quartz and iron oxides cause reddish, grey and white tints and veining. Hematite and iron cause red, pink and browns; limonite produces a yellow colouration and serpentine a deep, rich green.

NEXT PAGE:
The Panormos quarry sits in the north-western corner of the Cycladic island of Tinos; it has been active since 1911 and is one of only two Tinian quarries still operating today. The Panormos mine is known for its Tinos Green marble, a green stone streaked with white veins, and Tinos Oasis, a jade-coloured rock identifiable by its golden channels. Mineralogically, the marbles extracted from Panormos belong to a group of minerals called the serpentines, named after the serpent for their patterned 'skin' and green colouration.

A shed at the Panormos quarry, 2018

Tinos Green marble at the Panormos quarry, 2018

PREVIOUS PAGE:

Tinos Green is a green marble of different hues, striated with white veins. It is a versatile material and can be used for both internal and external purposes such as in flooring and wall cladding, and to make seating, fireplaces, water fountains, pools and countertops. This marble is also called Green of Tinos, Green Tinos, Tinos Marmor, Tinos Verde, Verde Tinos and Panormos Green.

NEXT SPREAD:

LEFT: Tinos Oasis is a green marble with golden veins. It too has many uses, both internal and external, such as in flooring, wall cladding, mosaics, water fountains, pools and countertops. This marble is also called Oasis Green, Verde Oasis, Verde Tropicus and Verde Tropical.

RIGHT: The earliest evidence of quarrying dates to prehistoric times in the Cyclades and predates the use of metals. Traces of ancient quarries can still be found around the Aegean, for example in Naxos, where extraction burgeoned during the early Archaic period. Greece's earth is rich in the minerals that make up marble. It is estimated that 75% of the country's landmass is marble-bearing. There are around 500 active quarries operating in Greece today, 10% of which are found on islands in the Cyclades and around 80% in northern Greece.

Tinos Oasis marble at the Panormos quarry, 2018

Blocks of marble being shaped from the vast wall of marble at the Panormos quarry, 2018

Marble blocks against a marble wall at the Panormos quarry, 2018

PREVIOUS PAGE:

Marble is heavy, weighing from 2.6 to 2.8 tonnes per cubic metre. It is a sought-after material in architecture as it is solid, hard-wearing in the right conditions, and can withstand great weight. It is also a material that absorbs and reflects light, and white marble is prized for its translucent qualities. As a sculptural material, marble is soft and workable, able to bear details and shadows.

NEXT SPREAD:

LEFT: Traditionally, marble extraction was performed manually with the use of wooden wedges, water, ropes, picks and shovels. For large-scale projects, the extraction and transportation of marble would have required a large and skilled workforce and was, in and of itself, a colossal feat.

RIGHT: Today, machines are used for industrial marble extraction, including diamond-tipped drill bits, diamond wire machines, hydraulic jacks, stone crushers and tractors. The quickening of technological advances in the last century has resulted in the rise of super quarries.

Workers at the Panormos quarry, 2018

An electric saw at the Panormos quarry, 2018

A view of the roads cut into the Panormos quarry, 2018

PREVIOUS PAGE:

Modern marble extraction begins by taking core samples to determine the best place to start digging a quarry. Once a site has been chosen, the surrounding earth is removed to reveal the marble wall. The wall is then cut into to extract individual blocks, which then are cut again into smaller units for different architectural or artistic uses.

NEXT SPREAD:

LEFT: As a material, marble is strong and durable, but also fragile. If a slab is struck at a specific angle, along its natural fissures and veins, it can easily break. This makes it vulnerable during extraction, but also when it is being transported, crafted and sculpted.

RIGHT: Marble extracted from Tinos has been used since the Archaic period to build structures all throughout the Mediterranean. Today, it is used both locally and internationally.

A fractured marble wall at the Panormos quarry, 2018

Large blocks of marble at the Panormos quarry, 2018

Marble offcuts and marble dust, 2018

Slabs of marble at the Panormos quarry, 2018

PREVIOUS SPREAD:

LEFT: Marble byproducts are used for a wide range of purposes. Crushed marble, for example, is used as an agricultural soil treatment to reduce acidity, to whiten paper, to create paint pigments, as a calcium supplement in animal feed and even to make antacids such as Tums and Alka-Seltzer.

RIGHT: It is thought that large structures made from marble were rare in the Archaic period due to a law made by Solon (c. 630–560 BCE), which prohibited structures that could not be completed within three days by ten men. Solon was a lawmaker and poet credited for laying the foundations for Athenian democracy.

NEXT PAGE:

Marble sculpting is so integral to the Tinian cultural identity that it was granted UNESCO Intangible Heritage status in 2015. The hilltop village of Pyrgos is where many of the island's marble sculptors live and work; here, they transform marble from rock to material to artefact. According to legend, Tinos was initiated into marble craft by the infamous sculptor and architect Phidias (c. 480–430 BCE). On Phidias' way to the nearby island of Delos, strong winds forced his ship to shelter at Tinos. He stayed a while and taught the craft of marble to the locals.

The hilltop village of Pyrgos, 2018

A shrine made of marble at the Panagia, Our Lady of Tinos, 2018

PREVIOUS PAGE:

The Panagia, Our Lady of Tinos, displays the use of marble in dedication to the divine. This is Greece's most important Marian shrine, as important to Greek Orthodox Christians as Lourdes in France is to Catholics. The church, and the 'miraculous icon' which inspired its construction, is said to protect those at sea and to heal the sick. The marble used to build the church comes from the nearby island of Delos, itself an extremely sacred site: a place of pilgrimage for the Ancient Greeks as the birthplace of Apollo, god of healing, divine distance, music and art; and his twin sister Artemis, goddess of wild animals, the hunt and vegetation.

NEXT SPREAD:

LEFT: Pyrgos is a living museum of marble in use, evident in street furniture, street signs and gutters. Even the village bus stop is made from solid marble. When Athens was established as the capital of modern Greece in 1834, following the Greek War of Independence, Tinian marble artists and craftspeople were invited to create and decorate many of its new landmarks such as the Zappeion, the National Archeological Museum, the University of Athens, the Athens Academy and the church of Zoodochos Pigi.

RIGHT: Many renowned marble artists and craftspeople have come from Tinos. Perhaps the most notable sculptor of modern Greece is Yannoulis Chalepas, born in Pyrgos in 1851. His family home in Pyrgos is now the Chalepas Museum, and displays his works and personal items. Chalepas' life was marked by his ongoing struggles with mental health, which he externalised by destroying his works and making several attempts to take his own life. At the age of 27, a few months after he created *Sleeping Girl*, which is pictured on the cover of this book, Chalepas suffered a major breakdown.

Marble bus stop in Pyrgos, 2018

The Chalepas Museum in Pyrgos, 2018

Framed sketches by Yannoulis Chalepas at the Chalepas Museum in Pyrgos, 2018

PREVIOUS SPREAD:
Yannoulis Chalepas was committed to the psychiatric hospital in Corfu by his family at the age of 27, where he stayed for 14 years until his father's death. His mother then took him back to Tinos where he worked as a shepherd. During this period of confinement and isolation, Chalepas was strongly discouraged from creating works as his mother blamed art for his mental condition. When she died in 1916, Chalepas returned to his craft, first in Tinos and later in Athens, right up until his death in 1938. In 1925, Chalepas' works were exhibited by the Academy of Athens, and in 1927 he received the Academy's Award for Excellence in Arts and Letters.

NEXT PAGE:
The earliest traces of marble use in human culture date back to the Late Neolithic Age (5300–4500 BCE). The most iconic objects found all across the Aegean – figurines of women made from white marble – are dated to the early Cycladic period (2800–2300 BCE). Some say these objects represent fertility; others speculate that they were placed with the dead as entertainment for the afterlife; others still suggest the figures depict goddesses. The School of Fine Arts in Pyrgos was established relatively recently, in 1955, and aims to teach marble craft and prepare students for further artistic study. The curriculum consists of five courses – marble carving, sculpture, painting and drawing, architectural design and art history.

A classroom at the School of Fine Arts in Pyrgos, 2018

NEXT PAGE:
Students from all across Greece come to attend the School of Fine Arts and each year, two graduates are automatically accepted to the Athens School of Fine Arts. In this way, the school and Tinos continue to feed Greece's marble culture beyond the island's shores.

Marble portraits at the School of Fine Arts, 2018

Friezes and sculptural works at the School of Fine Arts, 2018

A window crowded with marble portraits at the School of Fine Arts, 2018

PREVIOUS SPREAD:

LEFT: The School of Fine Arts is run by director Leonidas Chalepas. Leonidas divides his time between teaching the sculpture course and his own artistic practice as an accomplished sculptor working with a wide range of materials. His marble works use the material and craft to tell contemporary narratives. He remembers each of his students, the details of their work and where they are today.

RIGHT: Traditionally, marblecraft was often passed down over generations of marble cutters, artisans and artists. Working with marble was a practice dominated by men. In fact, there are only a handful of written accounts that describe female artists of any kind in Ancient Greece. Today, almost a quarter of the apprentices in Tinos are women.

NEXT PAGE:

Marble craftsman Petros Marmarinos' grandfather was an artist who also owned a small construction company in Istanbul (then, Constantinople). When the Greeks were exiled from the city, the family left for Athens and began to visit their village of familial origin, Pyrgos.

Petros Marmarinos working in his studio in Pyrgos, 2018

Calipers at Petros Marmarinos' studio, 2018

Marble works, materials and tools at Petros Marmarinos' studio, 2018

PREVIOUS SPREAD:

LEFT: Many of the sculpting tools used to work marble today are the same as those used in antiquity. Roughing out a marble block is done with a mallet and chisel with either a pointed or squared-off end. The work is given a more precise form with finer chisels: a claw or toothed chisel and a flat chisel. A drill is used throughout to cut the outlines of reliefs and to drill holes for eyes and ears, and channels that distinguish hair from skin and cloth. Once the detail is complete, a work is finished by smoothing it out with a rasp and it is polished with pumice, emery or sand. Finally, the form might be painted with a mix of pigments, wax and oil.

RIGHT: Petros was born and raised in Pyrgos. His surname, Marmarinos, means 'made of marble'. He says that he can't imagine how hard it would be to work as a professional marble sculptor today. "It's very time-consuming and it's hard on your body. As soon as I enter my studio I enter a vortex, I am that focused. I'll start work in the morning and at some point I realise that it's already evening. I get obsessed; it feels like entrapment; it becomes my only priority. I can't stop until I finish. So, everything else in my life takes second place."

NEXT PAGE:

Petros studied at the School of Fine Arts in Pyrgos but never felt the urge to continue his formal education. He says that Pyrgos gives him everything he needs – natural and architectural beauty and culture steeped in the old traditions of marble.

The marble yard at Petros Marmarinos' studio, 2018

NEXT PAGE:
Petros works from his orange-scented, north-facing garden studio and stays true to the classic techniques of marble craft. He says, "It's hard being a sculptor but I will never regret my choice. This form of communication is the most powerful of all."

The marble yard and outdoor work space at Petros Marmarinos' studio, 2018

Marble work by Michail Saltamanikas in his studio, 2018

Michail Saltamanikas in his studio in Pyrgós, 2018

PREVIOUS SPREAD:

LEFT: Michail Saltamanikas describes his relationship with marble as "love beyond technique and knowhow. It consumes my existence." He says that he often finds a piece of marble that guides him to the final form of the work. He once became so enchanted by a piece of marble glittering at the bottom of the sea that he returned to dive for it, painstakingly hauling it to the surface over the course of an entire day.

RIGHT: Michail was born in Pyrgos and began his artistic career sculpting wood before working in marble under the guidance of his grandfather, master sculptor Lazaros Artemios Valakas. He graduated from the School of Fine Arts in Pyrgos and has been working from his studio in Pyrgos since 1997.

NEXT PAGE:

Lambros Diamantopoulos says his craft has always been "the balm of his life". He graduated from the School of Fine Arts in Pyrgos in 1971 and was an apprentice to the renowned Tinian sculptor, Dimitrios Filippotis. Filippotis was such a prolific marble sculptor that he was nicknamed "marmarophagus" – marble-eater. In 1978, Lambros started his own studio and began creating and restoring marble works.

Lambros Diamantopoulos in his studio in Pyrgos, 2018

Lambros Diamantopoulos' tools at his studio, 2018

PREVIOUS PAGE:

When asked if his own children will continue the marble sculpting tradition, Lambros replies, "No. The craft is difficult; it takes time and patience. You might work on one piece for days or even a month. Most young people nowadays find it difficult to focus on something like that for a long time. You have to love it. It's a calling."

Marble artworks and tools at Lambros Diamantopoulos' studio, 2018

PREVIOUS SPREAD:
Lambros touches his tools and the marble blocks with respect and a certain softness. At the door of his studio he gives a kind smile and says, "Come back and visit whenever you want."

ATHENS
CHRIS KONTOS

Marble bath and artefacts in an Athenian apartment, 2021

PREVIOUS PAGE:
The area that Athens now occupies has been inhabited since the Neolithic period (c. 7000–3200 BCE). Athens is one of the oldest cities in the world, with a recorded history of over 3,400 years. It has been made and remade since its ancient origins – from the Roman to the Byzantine empires, Ottoman rule, the reign of King Otto to modern times. Marble has been used to communicate Greek identity through art and architecture throughout these cultural upheavals. In Athens, it seems that the city's very bones are made of marble.

NEXT PAGE:
The Parthenon was built during the second half of the fifth century BCE as a home to Athena, goddess of wisdom, patroness and protector of the city. Under her pseudonym, Ergane, Athena is also patroness to marble and bronze workers, potters and weavers. The Parthenon was created with 25,000 tonnes of raw material by close to 500 artisans and over 20,000 unskilled labourers. It is made from the fine-grained white Pentelic marble, which has been quarried since the first millennium BCE from Mount Pentelikon, north of Athens. The quarry is now reserved exclusively for conservation work on the remaining monuments of the Acropolis.

A view of the Parthenon from Koukaki, 2021

A marble column of the Parthenon, 2013

PREVIOUS PAGE:
The monuments that sat on the Acropolis suffered many vicissitudes over the centuries: arson by Germanic tribes in the late third or fourth century; the destruction of artworks by Christian Greeks in the sixth century; its reassembly into a Frankish tower by the Duchy of Athens in the late 14th century; conversion into a mosque by the Ottomans in the early 1460s; and direct attack by the army of the Republic of Venice in 1687. The worst transgression, perhaps, was the removal of half of the Parthenon's surviving sculptures by the Earl of Elgin in the early 19th century. Although the Greek government first made a formal request to return the 'Parthenon Marbles' in 1983, they remain confined to the British Museum in London, United Kingdom.

NEXT SPREAD:
The practice of marble engraving as a method of broadcasting information to the public dates back to antiquity, when inscriptions were made in public spaces to communicate laws to citizens. In Greece, and especially in Athens, white marble was favoured for this practice, due to the clarity of the engraved lettering.

A marble bench on Dionysiou Areopagitou Street in the Acropolis area, 2018

A decorated marble wall in central Athens, 2018

PREVIOUS PAGE:

Marble's presence in Athens can feel overwhelming for the people who work with it. A material of such significant weight, both physical and cultural, can slow down building processes. Marble artefacts are uncovered during excavations for new buildings; the material must also be transported, unloaded and placed for a new build or renovation. On Entropy, a marble atelier operating between Athens and London, put it simply: "Marble can be both a precious rarity and a burdensome ubiquity."

NEXT SPREAD:

LEFT: Despite its relative durability, marble weathers and decays under certain conditions. These include rainwater acidified by carbon dioxide; sulfur dioxide and nitrogen oxides created by air pollution; moisture; air pollutants such as soot; hydrocarbons and metallic oxides; and bacteria, algae, fungi and lichens. Cracks can also form due to heat stress and from physical disruption such as earthquakes.

RIGHT: Athenians have been burying their dead at the site of the ancient cemetery since the early Bronze Age (2700–2000 BCE), and it was a formal cemetery from the late Bronze Age until the Roman period (31 BCE–180 CE). Outside the necropolis, the Sacred Gate marked the beginning of the Sacred Way and a procession known as the Eleusinian Mysteries. This was a celebration of the reunion of the goddess Demeter with her daughter Persephone – a set of secret rites, ceremonies and psychoactive drugs was enacted and imbibed by all social classes in this celebration for over two millennia. These were some of the few rituals that transcended social hierarchies.

Ancient weathered marble on view in the National Archeological Museum's yard, 2021

Marble tombs at the Ancient Cemetery in Kerameikos, 2021

An icon of Saint Paraskevi framed in marble at the chapel of Agia Paraskevi in central Athens, 2021

PREVIOUS PAGE:
The chapel of Agia Paraskevi was built during the Ottoman period. Previously controlled by the Byzantine emperor, Constantine XI Palaeologus, Constantinople fell to the Ottomans in 1453. The emperor died on the day of the battle, inspiring the 'Marmaromenos Vasilias' legend – that the emperor had turned to marble but would one day return and liberate his people. The Ottomans, of Islamic faith, created the millet system to govern different religions under its rule. The Greek Orthodox Christians belonged to the Rūm millet, second only to the ruling Muslim millet. They were allowed relative autonomy to conduct their religious affairs.

NEXT SPREAD:
LEFT: The Metropolitan Cathedral of the Annunciation, popularly known as the Mētrópolis, is the cathedral church of the Archbishopric of Athens and all of Greece. Its construction began in 1842 under the Austrian architect Theophil Hansen, in a neoclassical design. It was completed 20 years later by Dimitris Zeppos in the Greek–Byzantine style using marble from 72 demolished churches. The Byzantine Empire prized certain marbles, even above gold. The stone dominates the exteriors and interiors of churches built during this era, its presence even more pervasive than the empire's legendary iconography.

RIGHT: Its name, the First Cemetery of Athens, is misleading: this is the first cemetery built in independent modern Athens but not the first cemetery in the city – a designation that belongs to Kerameikos. It is made almost entirely of white Pentelic marble. Marble craftsmen were invited from Tinos by the Mayor of Athens to build neoclassical tombs, angels of mourning, temples, sarcophagi, urns, busts, standing and seated sculptures, ornate crosses and monuments. Many of the works for this new necropolis emulated the tombs of the Ancient Cemetery in Kerameikos. Some of the more prominent monuments and stelae were brightly painted; traces of red, black, blue and green pigments are still visible today.

Decorative pot at the Metropolitan Cathedral of the Annunciation at Metropolis Square, 2021

Sculpture at the Pesmazoglou family mausoleum
by Italian sculptor Francesco Jerace (1853–1937) at the First Cemetery of Athens, 2018

The Melas mansion at Kotzia Square, 2018

Water fountain in the garden of the Mesogeia Athens Vorres Museum in Paeania, 2021

PREVIOUS SPREAD:

LEFT: Following the Greek War of Independence, there was a renewed nationalist interest in historically Greek architectural styles. Classical architecture of Ancient Greece and Rome was revived with neoclassical architecture. The Melas mansion, designed by Ernst Ziller and built in 1874, is an example of this style, characterised by symmetry, minimalism and references to the Classical era, mostly through decorative marble elements such as caryatids. The building is now home to the Cultural and Administrative Centre of the National Bank of Greece.

RIGHT: The Ancient Greeks were the first to construct aqueducts and gravity fountains. These fountains used a mix of gravity and pressure to move water up from under the ground, and supplied drinking water to locals. Greek fountains were made of stone or marble with water flowing through bronze pipes. The end of the pipe was often sculpted into the shape of a lion's head, or that of another animal. In the sixth century BCE, the Athenian ruler Peisistratos (600–527 BCE) built the central fountain of Athens in the main square, drawn from a spring named Kallirhoè (beautiful flow). The fountain was named Enneacrounos, after its nine spouts.

NEXT PAGE:

This building at 17 Dionysiou Areopagitou Street was designed by architect Vasileios Kouremenos (1875–1957) in the 1930s. It is a small block of apartments that features motifs favoured by the French École des Beaux-Arts, from which Kouremenos graduated in 1904. In a funny ouroboric loop, the école's curriculum took Ancient Greek and Roman art as its starting point. The building's façade features marble columns, caryatids and decorative mosaics depicting ancient themes.

A caryatid at 17 Dionysiou Areopagitou Street in the Acropolis area, 2018

Façade of 37 Dionysiou Areopagitou Street in the Acropolis area, 2018

PREVIOUS PAGE:
A little further down Dionysiou Areopagitou Street, at number 37, is another example of Kouremenos' work: the façade pictured here is a marble patchwork of grey, green and pink stone. Kouremenos' combination of the classical and the contemporary is an example of the art deco style with a distinctly Greek identity in terms of materiality, aesthetic, design and technique. Dionysiou Areopagitou Street was first mapped in 1857 and then redesigned in 1955 by the revered architect Dimitris Pikionis, who was responsible for the marble-paved pathways and landscaping leading up to the Acropolis.

NEXT SPREAD:
LEFT: The marble column is perhaps one of the most pervasive elements of Ancient Greek architecture, and the most recognisable feature of Greco-Roman design. Doric, Ionic and Corinthian columns can be found in many contemporary buildings, especially in the Western world. Originally, they served as the exterior pillars of sacred buildings such as temples; today, they are frequently seen in public buildings.

RIGHT: A caryatid is a female figure sculpted from marble that serves as an architectural support in the place of a column or pillar. The most famous caryatids are those of the Erechtheion in the Acropolis, built to house the statue of Athena Polias. The caryatids that support the House of the Caryatids pictured here were created in 1880 by the house's owner, Aeginian sculptor Ioannis Karakatsanis (1857–1906), who modelled the sculptures on his wife Xanthi and her sister Evdokia.

An Ionic column in central Athens, 2018

House of the Caryatids on 45 Agion Asomaton Street in Psyrri, 2021

The Iliad (1965), marble relief by Paris Prekas for an office building in central Athens, 2018

PREVIOUS PAGE:

By the 1960s, many neoclassical residential buildings were being demolished, making way for modern apartments and office buildings. This office building at 2 Karagiorgi Servias Street was commissioned from architect Ioannis Vikelas (1931–) by the National Bank. Vikelas designed many of the tall buildings in Athens during this period. Painter and sculptor Paris Prekas (1926–1999) was commissioned to create work for the foyer space in 1965. Prekas' *The Iliad* is an installation of 15 white marble slabs that depict heroes from the epic ancient poem of the same name.

NEXT SPREAD:

LEFT: Banks have made their home in many of the old marble-clad buildings in Athens. The material communicates stability, power and professionalism. Beyond these aesthetic cues there are also functional reasons to use marble in large buildings of this kind. Marble façades regulate the exchange of heat, light and air between the internal and the external environment, optimising thermal performance in summer and winter.

RIGHT: Between 1930 and 1990, thousands of apartment buildings, known as polykatoikia, were constructed in Athens. This swift development followed the antiparochi land-for-apartment exchange law of 1929 which sought to accommodate the arrival of refugees following population exchanges between Greece and Turkey. It also assisted arrivals after Nazi occupation and the civil war of the 1940s. This rapid urbanisation changed the city's shape and makeup; its boundary lines swelled and many of its low-density neoclassical buildings were replaced with five- to seven-storey polykatoikies. Architects had limited involvement in these postwar constructions, which resulted from a unique form of bottom-up development led by land owners and self-taught construction managers.

Alpha Bank on the corner of Aiolou and Sofokleous Streets in central Athens, 2021

A polykatoikia on Vassilissis Sofias Avenue in central Athens, 2021

A polykatoikia on Rigillis Street in the Rigillis district, 2018

Pedestrian tiles along Aiolou Street in central Athens, 2021

PREVIOUS SPREAD:

LEFT: The aesthetic of the polykatoikia falls into three distinct periods: the ornamentation and opulence of the 1950s constructions; the cheaper and more minimalist approach of the 1970s; and the buildings of the 1990s, which feature next to no decorative elements at all. The vertical social stratification of the polykatoikia is well established. Ground floors were (and continue to be) occupied by retail services, while the upper floors rose to mirror a social 'ascension', occupied by 'higher' social classes all the way up to the penthouse flats at the top. The ground floor of the polykatoikia is the meeting place of these different social classes, where they encounter each other on a daily basis.

RIGHT: Aiolou Street begins at the Tower of the Winds, a clock tower made of Pentelic marble and named after the wind god, Aiolos. It was the first street in Athens to be paved. In 1833, architects Stamatis Kleanthis and Eduard Schaubert designed Aiolou Street as part of planning for the new independent capital. It was conceived as a pedestrian commercial street, a continuation of its market legacy which stretches back to antiquity. Excavations in the 1970s uncovered seven layers of road laid one on top of the other.

NEXT PAGE:

The maroon marble, Rosso Antico, was mainly quarried in the south of Greece, at the Mani Peninsula in the Peloponnese. It was first mined during the late Bronze Age, from the Minoan (3000–1100 BCE) to the Mycenaean period (c. 1600–1100 BCE) up until the Hellenistic period (323–33 BCE) when it was used to create stelae dedicated to the local Spartan goddess, Artemis Orthia. It was also used extensively during the Roman period (31 BCE–180 CE), its reddish-purple colour associated with nobility.

Rosso Antico marble in a foyer in central Athens, 2018

Street sign on Patissison Street in central Athens, 2021

The Athens Conservatoire, 2018

PREVIOUS SPREAD:

LEFT: In Greece, road signs date back to antiquity. The first road signs were known as hermai (ἑρμαῖ, 'block of stone') and were usually comprised of a sculpture with a head (and sometimes a torso), placed on a quadrangular pillar about the size of a human body. These hermai often had male genitalia. The messenger god and protector of wayfarers, Hermes, was a common motif on hermai, and they were often placed to mark gates and doorways. Simplified marble street signs like the one on Patission Street were common in Athens during the 19th century.

RIGHT: The Athens Conservatoire, commonly referred to as Odeion, was part of Ioannis Despotopoulos' (1903–1992) plan for a grand cultural centre in Athens. The design included an 1,800-seat opera house, an orchestral and ballet hall, a circular theatre, a playhouse for experimental theatre, an extension to the National Gallery, a new Byzantine museum and a church. The Conservatoire is the only building ever to be realised from the ambitious plan, but delays and cost constraints halted the partially constructed project in 1976, and it was only completed in 2017. Despotopoulos is the only Greek architect to have studied under Walter Gropius, the founder of the Bauhaus school.

NEXT PAGE:
This large-format terrazzo flooring is set within a series of rectangular, circular and semicircular slabs of Kokkinarás marble coupled with a light grey terrazzo with a white aggregate. The marble was mined 16 kilometres northeast of the city. The slabs were digitally mapped and then shaped with a waterjet cutter, cut without waste, and the offcuts were broken up and used elsewhere in the apartment. This work is part of an apartment refurbishment in a polykatoikia built in the 1950s.

Large-format terrazzo flooring in an apartment in Kypseli, 2021

Modern terrazzo flooring made from salvaged marble in an apartment in Kypseli, 2021

A residential foyer laid with smoky-veined black marble tiles on Rigillis Street, 2018

PREVIOUS SPREAD:
LEFT: This terrazzo flooring is made from smashed fragments of marble considered impure – flush with cracks and defects. The floor's surface treatment acts as an expansion join and allows the terrazzo floor to swell and contract without cracking. This work is part of the same refurbishment as that on page 121.

RIGHT: Both marble tiles and terrazzo floorings have been used in neoclassical and modern buildings for their shared durability and aesthetic. There is an important difference between the two, however – pricing. Terrazzo makes use of marble offcuts, stone aggregates and cement and is by far the cheaper option. As such, its use was an indication of the socioeconomic position of a building's intended inhabitants.

NEXT PAGE:
Athens' many marble yards are full of marble sinks, baths, columns, steps, slabs, tiles and blocks. These are motley relics from modern Greece, leftovers from quarries or salvaged from demolished buildings. Since the global financial crisis, there are a number of apartments that have been abandoned and left in decay, their owners unable to pay land taxes. The yards offer ways to sensitively refurbish and renovate these old buildings that have been left behind. This bathroom in a postwar polykatoikia in Koukaki built in 1979, includes a bath made from Aliveri marble and walls made of Kokkinarás and Dionysos marble.

A patchwork of reclaimed marble in a residential apartment in Koukaki, 2021

A souvenir shop in Monastiraki, 2021

PREVIOUS PAGE:

In the crowded and narrow Pandrossou and Iphestou streets in the Monastiraki district of Athens, souvenir shops sell anything that could be considered Greek. Copies of ancient marble statues made from plaster or alabaster are among the most popular items. These cheaply made mass-produced imitations of some of Greece's most iconic marble statues are testament to the importance of the Greek tourism industry. They recall the models made of plaster, clay or wax used by some marble sculptors as working references before committing final marks to stone.

NEXT PAGE:

In a new series of investigations by Athens-based artist Theodore Psychoyos, these marble furniture pieces are based on function and balance. The verticals are made from core samples, the first stage in the process of extracting marble. The horizontal crusts are not salvaged marble per se; Theodore describes them as "marble that hasn't yet found its purpose". The marbles are sourced from a family-run quarry that supplied marble for use in modern Athens. Some of the pieces were extracted as long as 80 years ago. Each piece has a patina, created by fungi, bacteria, water and the other elements with which the material came into contact during its time in the marble yards, while it was waiting to be put to use.

Marble shelves by Theodore Psychoyos, 2021

AFTERWORD
NADINE MONEM

In what way can we know a stone, its character and its movements? How can we understand a material that moves according to a register of time outside of the reach of the human imagination? Humans have a problem with time. Many of us can only stretch our stories back for a few of our short lifespans, and hardly move them forward even one. In order to understand our relation to other forces in the natural world, to a material like marble, we attempt to piece together time and its gestures through our small measures – a patchwork that falls apart when stretched too far, when it is pulled across too many years. We struggle to hold time in this way, in the way that stone can hold time.

To trace marble's origins we have to somehow stretch our minds back hundreds of millions of years. Back to when most of the earth was covered in water and moved according to the choreography of waves. Back then, beneath those waves, Permian sea creatures – trilobites, nautiloids, ammonites, with their soft bodies and hard shells – drifted in the sparse waters. When they ceased their drifting, their soft bodies would dissolve, or be metabolised by other soft bodies, and their hard shells would sink through the dark waters and settle on the ocean floor. The bodies would accumulate, organised slowly by the attentive drift of the water. The great pressure of the ocean pressed down on them, and pressed them together, to form rivers of limestone. Other geologic material – sand, quartz, silica – snaked its way through the stone, altering its colour and behaviour. Over time this limestone was itself pulled down, closer to the molten heat of the earth's core, where it was folded in on itself, transformed.

The bodies that had settled, one by one, re-crystallised into a phantom snapshot of their particular and contingent place and time. Or, put another way, a series of accidents was fired hard by heat and pressure and made monumental. But it is only when this metamorphosed now-marble was eventually thrust up to the earth's surface some millennia after its making that our human eyes could encounter it, and could take it up in the theatre of our culture.

***

There is a legend that the island of Tinos, where Chris Kontos took many of the photographs in this book, became one of the most important sites of marble craft in the world because of another enduring accident of history. The story is that around 2,500 years ago the Greek sculptor Phidias, famous for crafting some of antiquity's most revered marble sculptures, was on his way to Delos when his ship was forced to shelter at Tinos because of bad weather. While he rode out the storm, he spent time with the local marble workers on the island, sharing his craft. Whatever was shared during that short time became part of the culture on the island, still visible today everywhere one happens to walk. Carved marble is evident all over the villages of the island, even in the bus stops, the street signs, the gutters, the graffiti etched into (and not painted on) the stone. Whether or not the legend is true, it seems inevitable that Tinos would have a long and integral cultural attachment to marble, given the island is built upon a thick spine of the stone in varieties that range from dove-white to the most verdant green.

The lines we perceive in the stone's exposed face are actually loops so vast that their grand arcs stretch for miles underground. Once this ground has been removed, once the trees, the soil, the rocks have been stripped away and all that is left is the shocked face of the opened earth, the great labour of extracting (or in the Greek, εκμεταλλεύονται, 'exploiting') the marble can begin. The stone is parsed into volumes that the human mind can make sense of and the human hand can manipulate. Holes are drilled down, or drilled in, and diamond-studded copper wire is threaded through to cut precise fragments from the vast stone. Whole mountains have been sheared off in this way, slab by slab.

The marble workers carefully traverse the changing elevations and extensions of the quarry, tracing the markings that suggest treasures buried deep underground, or fresh dangers lurking ahead. They keep the marble wet while they cut, so that the stone, and the machines used to cut it, don't overheat while they work. The water slips over the new angles of the quarry in milk-coloured rivers, winding its way to other bodies of water, eventually taking the marble sediment all the way back to the ocean. If water is not used in the cutting of marble, the incisions can become noxious. The marble dust rises in heavy clouds and finds its way into the open airways of the quarry workers, settling in the moist darkness of throats and lungs, and remaining there – agitated.

Because marble moves more slowly than our senses can perceive, it is true to say that it cannot insert itself into our moral conversations, not in a way that we can hear. But each volume of the marble we find today is finite, its composite beings having left the earth millennia ago. And so, as a material available to exhaustion, marble does articulate a moral question in its own persistent register. Several types of Tinian marble are endangered, and at least one has become extinct. And with that extinction, a second death occurs.

The last traces of ancient life within the endless wave of the marble's form are lost forever.

***

From our human vantage point, inside of our small pocket of geological time, marble might appear passive, static, even silent, but the material quality of marble tells the story of its own movements, evidences its own long becoming. Even its translucency is evocative of its watery origins. Some of the most highly sought-out marble admits light far into its depths before reflecting it back, like the dark of the oceans in which it was first forged. This availability to light animates form, changing its character with the seasons, the time of day, with the shadows cast on its surface. It might have been this aliveness that first drew the early architects of culture to the stone as a material that can speak back to its surroundings.

The glow of reflected light, refracted through the spidery traces of deep history, captures the philosophical and spiritual imagination. It entices us to make marble a metaphor for our highest ideals of solidity, permanence, power – for the enduring imprint of human intention on the raw material of nature. Monuments to great figures of philosophy, theology or war have been carved in marble since antiquity, and these rising forms, larger than life, stand today as anxious claims to immortality commissioned by people who are long dead. Some of these claims now reside in museums, stored behind glass or protected by the softest velvet rope. As the ultimate expression of domination, there is a special relationship between marble and empire, from the Acropolis in Athens to Trajan's Column in Rome, to the interiors of Buckingham

Palace in London and the Capitol Building in Washington. It is also used in empire building in the modern context, in structures designed for the state's close relations – banks, universities, museums, places of worship. The first large hotel chain to open its doors in Athens, the Hilton, commissioned the Greek artist Yannis Moralis to carve a relief in its towering marble façade. Moralis elected to carve a series of ancient figures, suggestive of a text, or a message from the past. So intimate is the relation between marble and power that some artists have used the material to challenge the economy of meaning in which ideas of power are formed. Louise Bourgeois, in making her anti-monuments in marble, did not seek to make the stone rise up and out, but rather she carved in and down, using soft forms that suggest enclosure rather than extension, and leaving the exterior of the form roughly hewn, geological, knowable to itself.

***

In our impatience for eternity, it is easy to forget that marble is porous, vulnerable when taken from the folds of the earth. It readily accepts not only the material and conceptual gestures of human intention etched into its body, but also the things we do not intend. It is a material that can easily stain, chip, crack, break apart. As Rachel Cusk writes here in this book, "human intentions must be subject to time: unless the bond with them is continually renewed, the vow to those intentions re-sworn, they will not be permitted to last." Marble that has been abandoned, or forgotten, is sometimes carefully salvaged and pieced together in new formal narratives, examples of which are shown in the pages of this book. There is something consoling about these forms, how they reference marble's prehistoric and recent past in sympathetic conversation. And the marble that does not find itself drawn into new human narratives continues to record the story of our indifference. Rains that were once so mild that they only darkened the surface of the stone now bear the traces of human industry, heavy with nitric or sulfuric acid. The calcite in marble's slow architecture dissolves when exposed to this acid rain, which bores holes in the polished surfaces, erases the fine detail imprinted by the human hand, and leaves the surface newly pocked and rough, sometimes unrecognisable. In our anxiety to assert the ways in which we are rational and not natural beings, we have inadvertently transformed ourselves into a geologic force that alters not only the surface of things, but also the way that all human and non-human beings interact.

***

In the spring of 1900, a group of Greek sponge divers were on their way to Tunisia, and like Phidias in the legend of Tinos, had to change course because the weather was too violent for sailing. They dropped anchor just off the coast of a small island called Antikythera and decided to dive for sponges there until the waters calmed enough to proceed. After a short while, one of the divers began to frantically tug on his line. When he was winched up, he appeared stricken, convinced he had stumbled upon dozens of partially concealed and decaying bodies reaching their limbs haphazardly out of the seabed. What he had actually found was the remains of a ship that had been wrecked 2,000 years before, sunk to the bottom of the Mediterranean Sea under the weight of several tons of plundered sculpture and scientific instruments. Some of these sculptures were formed in marble, and when they were finally pried from their watery resting place, they appeared chimeric. The parts of the forms that were nestled in the seabed were smooth, perfectly preserved, every detail of their carving bell-clear and precise. The exposed parts of the marbles had resumed their ancient conversation with the water, the waves loosening the surface of the stone into microscopic fragments, freeing the material to start a new cycle of becoming. To look at these sculptures, now housed in the Athens Archaeological Museum, is to see two registers of time – the human and the non-human – exist in each single object.

***

Marble could be said to carry its own message, the faint glimmer of extinction concealed within its form. Even in all of the exaltations of endurance it has been used to create, the bodies of beings that once dominated the earth exist there as sediment, transformed by time, acting as a *memento mori* gifted to one geologic epoch from another. Humanity will not exist long enough to intuit our last traces in marble's making of itself, to see how the movements of our human history will snake through the slow waving of the stone. We are not good at imagining a world without us, how we might also be transformed by the geologic register. Or, the prospect of that imagining is too discomforting to attempt. Perhaps, here, the ancient forms of the stone can be a comfort. Jenny Holzer once carved words of consolation in a modest marble bench, part of her *Survival Series* (1998). The words she carved were: "In a dream you saw a way to survive, and you were full of joy."

Απόσπασμα από τη *Ρωμιοσύνη*
Του Γιάννη Ρίτσου

Μαρμάρωσαν τὰ δέντρα, τὰ ποτάμια κ᾽ οἱ φωνὲς μὲς στὸν ἀσβέστη τοῦ ἥλιου.
Ἡ ρίζα σκοντάφτει στὸ μάρμαρο. Τὰ σκονισμένα σκοίνα.
Τὸ μουλάρι κι ὁ βράχος. Λαχανιάζουν. Δὲν ὑπάρχει νερό.
Ὅλοι διψᾶνε. Χρόνια τώρα. Ὅλοι μασᾶνε μία μπουκιὰ οὐρανὸ πάνου ἀπ᾽ τὴν πίκρα τους.

An extract from *Romiosini*
By Yannis Ritsos
Translated by Nikos Kalogeropoulos

Trees, rivers and voices turn to marble in
the sun's whitewash.
Roots trip on marble. Dust-laden mastic trees.
Mule and rock. All pant. There is no water.
All thirst. For years now. All chew a mouthful of sky to rise
above their bitterness.

ACKNOWLEDGEMENTS

The publisher would like to gratefully acknowledge the creative contributions of Rachel Cusk, Chris Kontos and Nadine Monem to *Marble in Metamorphosis*. We would like to thank Niki and Zoe Moskofoglou, of On Entropy, for their research into marble which has informed this book, and for facilitating inspiring relationships with the marble practitioners in Tinos. We thank sculptors Michail Saltamanikas, Lambros Diamantopoulos and Petros Marmarinos for sharing their craft and recollections and for their time during the production of the photographic series included in this book. Gratitude also to Leonidas Chalepas, the Director of the Panormos School of Fine Arts, for giving us his time and his insights on marble craft in the Tinian context. Finally, we would like to acknowledge our work and ongoing collaboration with architects Royffe Flynn, some of which appears on pages 121, 122 and 125 of this book.

CREDITS

(p.7) Excerpt from 'Mythistorema', by George Seferis, translated by Edmund Keeley, in *George Seferis: Collected Poems, 1924–1955* (Princeton University Press, 1995). (c) George Seferis and Edmund Keeley, reprinted by permission of Princeton University Press.

(p. 139) Excerpt from *Romiosini* by Yannis Ritsos (Kedros, 1961), translated by Nikos Kalogeropoulos. (c) Yannis Ritsos, reprinted by the generous permission of Mrs Eri Ritsou and Kedros Publishers.

CONTRIBUTORS

RACHEL CUSK is the author of memoirs *A Life's Work*, *The Last Supper* and *Aftermath*, the trilogy *Outline*, *Transit* and *Kudos*, nine other works of fiction, and *Coventry*, a book of essays. Her 2021 novel, *Second Place*, was shortlisted for The Booker Prize.

CHRIS KONTOS is an Athens-based photographer and the founder of *Kennedy Magazine*, a 'Biannual Journal of Curiosities' first published in 2013, now in its 13th edition.

NADINE MONEM is a Canadian writer of memoir and theory, her 2021 essay *Confidence Man* won runner-up for the Sewanee Review Nonfiction Contest. She is the founder of independent artists' book publisher, common-editions.

YANNIS RITSOS (1909–1990) is known as 'the great poet of the Greek Left', publishing more than 100 works over his lifetime, including essays, plays and collections of poetry. Ritsos was a vocal member of the Communist party and an active part of the Greek Resistance during World War II.

GEORGIOS SEFERIADES (pen name, GEORGE SEFERIS) (1900–1971) was a Greek poet, essayist and diplomat. He published 15 works of poetry and prose, and was awarded the Nobel Prize for Literature in 1963, the first Greek writer to be awarded the honour.

MOLONGLO

At its core, property development is the willing of architecture into being; from an abstraction of drawings and ideas into something to be touched, occupied and lived in. Molonglo is interested in theoretical discussions about the built environment and how these ideas can be applied in practice.

Molonglo's Athenian work seeks to advocate for the city and its inhabitants. To support it and them in engaging with opportunities, post-economic crisis, in gentle and appropriate ways. It is here we are driven to investigate this vernacular material and the appropriateness of its application in our work. It is a privilege to be working in this rich and textured city. It is through these projects that our interest in marble has been honed.

Molonglo publications endeavour to agitate within the property industry and take discussions about the complexity of development out of closed rooms and into the wider world. Current and forthcoming areas of interest include the built environment (new and old), ownership, custodianship and use of land, landscape and nature, human-led materials and processes, migration and narrative objects.

Essay author: Rachel Cusk
Photographer: Chris Kontos
Afterword author: Nadine Monem
Caption authors: Sophia Sapouna and Stéph Donse

Cover: *I Kimomeni* (Η Κοιμωμένη, 'Sleeping Girl') (1878), Tinian sculptor Yannoulis Chalepas' most widely known work. She lies in the First Cemetery of Athens, where Chalepas is also buried. Photograph by Chris Kontos.

Commissioning editor: Rachel Elliot-Jones
Designer: U-P
Copyeditor: Mel Campbell
Proofreader: Leanne Gu

Printer: Wilco Art Books
Photography reproduction: Colour and Books
Typeface: Laica A by Dinamo
Papers: Munken Pure Rough 100gsm, Munken Pure (Bioset) 90gsm, Munken Kristall Rough 100gsm, Munken Polar Rough 90gsm, Munken Print White 90gsm

Published by Molonglo
Collingwood VIC 3066, Australia
molonglo.com

ISBN 9780987634429
© 2022 Molonglo and individual authors

All rights reserved. No part of this publication may be reproduced, stored in a retrieval system, or transmitted, in any form or by any means, electronic, mechanical, recording or otherwise, without prior written permission from the publisher.